Support

The Key To "Meant All Health" Recovery

It's A Rap

A lifestyle Choice

By Olivia Johnson

ISBN: 9798504369877

Support

Sunshine

In the night

Knowing

It will be

Alright

Alone

Alone

Alone

This path to take

We need

To keep you

Just awake

Friends are good

That I know

That's what everyone

Told me sow

Distraught

Though

It Can Be

Difficult

For me

To See

A Conundrum

Peculiar though...

This is...

Lonely

Despite

The support

Around

No friends to see

Them to be found

There is a

Weakness in

This Soul of Mine

That does not

Even find a dime

Beyond care

I often feel

So ill

It's not even real

As if I can

Take the thrill

The thrill of friendship

That could be mine

All I know is

I feel ill

Yet I don't

Prise off

The fashion still

And I don't want to

Just sit still

Without support

I would not cope

Without support

I would just dope

With support

I am here to try

Even if

I feel like a spy

It takes ages

To recover

It takes ages

Just to see

What the hell

Has happened to me!

All I know

Is without Support

I would not do

What I ought

It keeps me on

The straight and

Narrow

So, I don't

Bend like an arrow

The problem with

An Empty life

Is it is full of strife?

You don't belong

You don't know why

But you still need

To give life a try

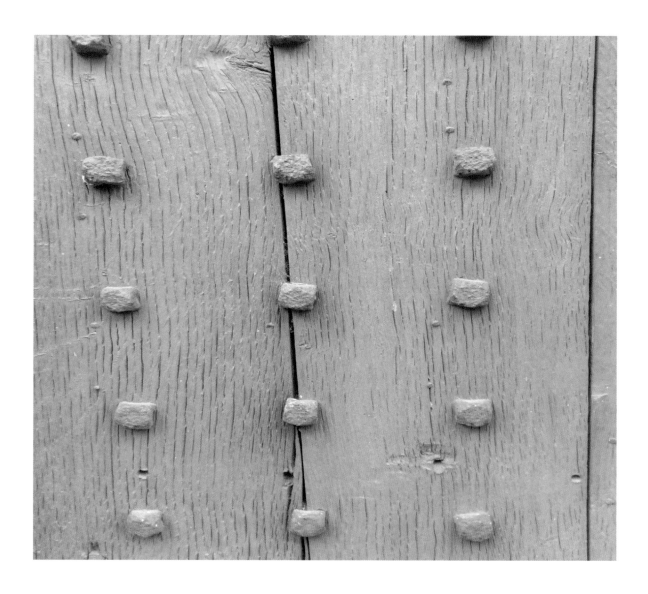

In earnest

I say to you

This is very

Very true

We need support

In every way

Someone to care

And let us know

That we are ok

Just to sow

We are ok

As we bumble

A long

We are ok

As we sing

Our Song

But what we need

Each Step of the Way

Is a friend

To let us pray

We feel

We cannot stay

Because we just might

Sway

We feel alone

And out of tone

We feel aloof

And on the hoof

There is so much

Involved in how

We are

There is so much

Involved in keeping

Us afloat

We just do not

Want to rock the boat

Without support

There is no hope

Then we will

Rock the boat

Be patient then

And understand

That we must learn

Our own free land

We must explore

Ourselves

To see our best

And then to see

All the rest

Our minds will

Help us

Through it all

Even if you

Don't feel that tall

We can support

Ourselves

As much to tell

That's what we need

Is your support

Of Deed

Just moving on

Is not enough

Then we will

Just gather dust

We will repeat the past

And not proceed

To a place

And not be freed

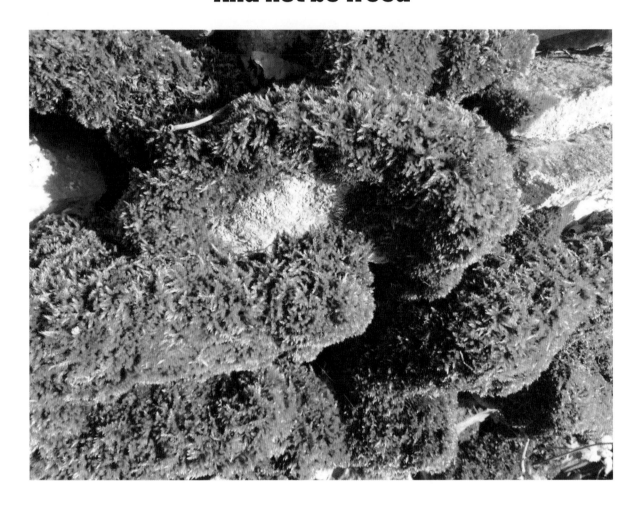

We need to

Support ourselves

And find out why

Why we see

And feel it too

That the sky

Is just not blue

So, your care

Is so precious

Without it who knows

What would happen

To us then

We might even

Just be Len

I think

As more people know

The journey it takes

To recover from the journey

That this illness takes

That people will realise

It was not just a mistake

They will come to know

How much we need

Their continual support

And not their heed

About the Author

The Author has found that the continual emotional and caring support from her brother

Provided a great and imperative foundation for her to be able to continually focus on her own

Self-development and Mental Health Recovery.

This in turn helped her to have the time and freedom to address her Mental Health Issues

through gaining Insight and Awareness and therefore to understand the underlying issues that

were causing her problems.

This took many decades of application.

Her brothers continual unwavering support also enabled her to carry on receiving the therapeutic

help from Certified and Professional Counsellors on a regular basis.

She feels it is a vital part of recovery to have some sort of supportive network throughout the

recovery journey to watch out for people suffering from Mental Health issues, and to keep life in

a normal balance. In her case it just happened to be her brother.

Disclaimer

This book is designed to provide information and motivation to its readers.

It is sold with the understanding that neither the publisher nor author are engaged to provide any type of

 psychological, legal or any other kind of professional mental health advice.

It is purely an expression of the author's own personal mental health journey and her or his reflections

upon it, and not that of the publisher.

Neither the publisher nor the author shall be liable for any physical, psychological, emotional,

 financial or commercial damages including, but not limited to special, incidental, consequential or other damages.

Our views and rights are the same.

The reader is responsible for their own choices, actions and results as a result of reading this book.

Printed in Great Britain
by Amazon

32044424R00023